WHAT WAS THAT VERSE AGAIN?

WHAT WAS THAT VERSE AGAIN?

Memory Improvement Methods For the Christian Worker

by BEN E. JOHNSON

illustrated by
Rod Burke

PUBLISHED BY
QUILL PUBLICATIONS.

DISTRIBUTED BY
MOTT MEDIA.
POST OFFICE BOX 236
MILFORD MICHIGAN 48042.

Published by
Quill Publications, Editorial Offices: 1260 Coast Village Circle,
  Santa Barbara, CA 93108
Distributed by
Mott Media, Post Office Box 236, Milford, Michigan 48042

Library of Congress Cataloging in Publication Data

Johnson, Ben E.
  What was that verse again?

  1. Mnemonics.   2. Bible—Memorizing.   I. Title.   BF385.J57
     153.1'4   76-21800

ISBN 0-916608-08-5

Cover Design and Illustrations by Rod Burke

FOR
ROBERT AND LORRAINE
McPHERSON

with thanks for many years of
exemplary devotion to God and to
family. Your years of consistent
Christian living have been a source of
strength for all who know you.

ACKNOWLEDGMENTS

I am grateful to Professor Ray Quiett, Chairman of the Department of Sociology, East Central University, Oklahoma, memory training specialist and creator of the AGP Modern Memory course, for his behind the scenes guidance, examples and creation of many of the original concepts discussed in this book. The author is also indebted to Professor Quiett for his willingness to read and evaluate this manuscript while still in preliminary form.

TABLE OF CONTENTS

INTRODUCTION

Often people ask me questions about memory and our ability to memorize. A common question for most people is, "Isn't ability to memorize related to IQ?" The answer is "no." The people with the highest intelligence do not necessarily have the best memories, nor do the people with the lowest IQs have the worst memories. Remember Einstein. He was a good example of the absent minded professor. In many areas his memory was spectacular for formulas, details, and various kinds of factual information. But at other times and in other areas his memory for details was very poor. This was probably simply a matter of interest or lack of interest as is the case with most of us. Even people with relatively low IQs sometimes develop phenomenal memories in certain limited areas. Regardless of IQ, you'll do fine. Read further.

Another question often asked is, "Do some people have what is commonly thought of as photographic memories?" The answer is still "no." And even if some people did have photographic memories, they probably wouldn't want them for any longer than a day or two because there are some built-in problems. This question is covered in more detail later in this book.

A third question is, "What about those fantastic memory demonstrations that we often see on television? Often a person will memorize the names and faces of an entire audience watching a live television program. Will I be able to do that if I read this book?" The answer is "maybe." If you think about it you will remember that the fantastic memory demonstrations you see on television are always the same demonstration and always by the same one or two people. Depending on the type of memory you wish to develop, you can develop relatively easily a fantastic memory for certain kinds of details. A person on television may appear to have a spectacular memory in all areas when really what he is doing is using memory training techniques in one highly practiced and very specialized area. This is rather impressive, but it is simply a combination of memory techniques that any person can develop, provided he wants to give special attention to that specialized kind of memorizing. This book will show you how to develop these areas.

The question is also asked, "Can you unconsciously destroy your memory ability?" Yes, you can. You cannot improve your memory by walking around and saying, "I have a bad memory." You will probably damage it, because as a result of saying this, you have a tendency to live up to your statements.

"Can a person consciously improve his memory?" Yes. The main difference among memories is that a few are trained while most are untrained.

And that's what this book is about. The Christian worker is under an obligation to use his strengths and talents in every way possible. The Christian with the trained memory is going to be much more useful in the Lord's work than the one who isn't trained.

And to train your memory is easy. This book will lead you carefully and systematically to a trained and productive memory. Don't skip around. Read straight through, practicing the techniques wherever you are asked to do so in these pages.

And when you are successfully using your new skills, send me a note and tell me about it, and I will rejoice with you.

Ben Johnson

WHAT WAS THAT VERSE AGAIN?

1
The Dangers of Misremembering and Forgetting

WHEN ASKED, the average person doesn't say he has a poor memory, he usually declares that he has a terrible memory. In actual fact, for many people, memory may even be nonexistent at some times for things which don't interest them, or at times when they are distracted, upset, or not feeling well.

Think of the number of times that you have been asked to stop at the store on the way home and pick up a few things: a pound of hamburger, a dozen eggs, a can of chili powder, and a tube of toothpaste. Now if you remembered to stop at all, you probably couldn't remember what it was you were supposed to pick up. So, you probably browsed up and down the aisles, looking at the items on the shelves, hoping that you would be reminded of the items. When you got home, and the shopping bag was unloaded, you watched with some dread and considerable apology as a pound of sugar, a dozen glazed donuts, a can of black pepper, and a tube of shampoo were placed on the table. Once again

19

you came close to remembering the list but, as someone has said (I can't remember who, or is it whom?), "Close only counts in horseshoes," or was it in marbles?

Ordinary lists of things like these very often escape us. Take, for example, wondering before we go to sleep at night if we locked the doors and put the cat out. Did we brush our teeth? Is that "thing" pulled out at the back of the alarm clock? And since we don't remember we get up and check! How many times have you turned on the radio or television to listen to the news so that you could hear the weather report, and then after you turned the set off you couldn't remember what the weatherman said?

Scores of jokes have been written about people with poor memories and the difficulties and misunderstandings that result. Did you hear the joke about the bridegroom who forgot which church he was to be married in? Oh, you did?—you think. Whole categories of people and professions are noted for their lack of ability to remember—from the absent minded professor to the "dumb blonde."

Some of life's most embarrassing moments have come to all of us because we couldn't remember a person's name at an important moment. It has even become dangerous lately to say, "How do you spell your last name again?" There are just too many Smiths and Joneses in the world. For the Christian worker it is not only embarrassing, it is destructive for your ministry if you forget a person's name whom you are attempting to reach with the Gospel. He is likely to take that as a sign of lack of care about him, and reject what you have to say.

On a practical level, think of the numbers of times we have misplaced items, forgotten to make phone calls, write letters, or pay bills. Think of the many telephone numbers and addresses we've forgotten, and the appointments we've missed, or have kept, but a day early. Think of the answers to questions, and the information we've forgotten for school tests, the poems, speeches, outlines, scripture verses and their references we no longer can remember. And what are the names of the 66 books of the Bible again, and what order are they in? Come to think of it, does Haggai come before or after Zephaniah?

The Difficulty of New Learning

Certainly it causes us problems when we forget things we once knew. But think of the difficulty and frustration we face in new learning situations when memorization comes hard for us. We are very often less than enthusiastic to begin such things as a scripture memorization program, because it is such work, and we forget so fast, even though we recognize its value. One of the things that the church has traditionally placed a high priority on, is scripture memorization. We see the value of "hiding" God's word in our hearts so that we might avoid sin (Psa. 119:11). Often Sunday schools and camps sponsor contests and offer prizes for young people who memorize scripture. The Bible advocates the memorizing of God's word. "And these words, which I command thee this day, shall be in thine heart" (Deut. 6:6). Furthermore, Psalm 1:2,3 tells us that it is when we meditate in God's word day and night that whatsoever we do will prosper. Romans 10:17 tells us that "faith cometh by hearing and hearing by the word of God." Most individual efforts as well as group programs of scripture memorization have been real "drags" if not outright failures, because memorization was work, and what scripture was memorized was quickly forgotten.

Inadequacy of Rote Memory or Repetition

The main reason that scripture memorization is such a difficult task and of such little value for most people, is that there has been no method of memorizing that was easy or interesting. Simple repetition or rote memory has been the only method known for memorizing, and it is inadequate. Simply repeating a verse, a fact, or a name over and over will eventually result in a memorized verse, fact, or name but only at great effort. And what about retention? Simply awful.

A person who is given a specific amount of material to learn in a brief period of time, and who attempts to remember it by simply going over and over the material, may find that he can memorize it. But if he is tested over the memorized material 24 hours later to determine what he remembers, he will be fortunate if he finds that he has retained 20% of what he "memorized" a day earlier.

The Photographic Memory

Because of these facts most of us yearn for what has been popularly called a photographic mind or photographic memory. Aside from the fact that this mythical super memory that operates with the speed and efficiency of a camera doesn't exist except in the imagination of writers and on television programs, you wouldn't want it if it did exist. There have been a few cases where something approaching a photographic mind has existed in a few people. These "gifted" people have nearly always had to be institutionalized because of severe physical and nervous breakdowns. These breakdowns came as a direct result of their ability to remember everything—and to forget nothing.

Forgetting Is Normal

Although we think we would enjoy being able to remember everything, it would be tragic. Every time you walked down a street and passed a picket fence, you would remember every picket—forever. Think of all the things that it is important that we forget: tragedies, pain, loss of loved ones, disappointments, hurt pride, and even pickets in the fence. God knew what he was doing when he built forgetting into us. It is for our own good. Forgetting is normal; unusual memory is abnormal.

But, forgetting as easily as we do is unnecessary; memory is the absence of forgetting. Developing an improved memory enables you to *selectively* remember what you want to without the dangers of the photographic memory.

Can Memory Be Improved?

There is a question that is often asked me and in a variety of ways, but it always comes across the same way. "I have had such a bad memory all my life, is it possible to improve it at my age?" The answer is "yes." There really is no such thing as a naturally bad memory. There are, however, an awful lot of *untrained* memories which are not being used. Memories can be classified as either trained or untrained. An untrained memory can be trained so that its abilities are used to capacity. Likewise however, a trained memory can become inefficient through disuse. As you continue reading this book, you will discover how to better manage your memory.

2
The Reasons People Don't Improve Their Memories

I N SPITE OF the fact that all people at least say they want to improve their memories, there is very little indication that many are actively doing so. There are many things that get in the way.

Physical Hindrances

There are relatively few physical roadblocks to memory improvement, but there are some. Some diseases not only affect the body but affect the mind directly. In addition, nearly any disease or injury tends to weaken a person's ability to remember.

Fatigue works the same way. As a person gets increasingly tired, he (and his memory) is less able to react actively to information. Many studies have shown that memory ability decreases as the day lengthens. Thus, a person is able to memorize much more rapidly in the morning than at night. Loss of sleep also lowers ability

27

to memorize. Alcohol and drugs cause poor retention and shorten the memory.

Old age often is associated with a loss of memory for recent events, but strangely enough old age often brings an improvement in memory for details of the distant past. We all know people who can describe with complete accuracy an event, a person or a day from 50 years ago.

Emotional and Psychological Hindrances

Nearly any strong feeling will lower our ability to remember. The emotion may be one of anger, frustration, grief, stage fright, hatred, joy, guilt, jealousy or even mild displeasure.

Often we actually think ourselves into a poor memory. There are those of us who find it easy to say, "I can't remember a thing, I have such a bad memory." We then begin to act in a way that is consistent with our self-image! We sometimes even come to glory in our perceived weakness of the mind, and are unwilling to change or to correct our personality quirk. Unconsciously, a person who laughingly declares that his memory is poor may actually find it necessary to prove it by forgetting things. But, what most chronic "forgetters" don't realize is that having a bad memory is not a particularly good quality to develop. In fact, family and friends may find it particularly undesirable, and it certainly does not contribute to success or enjoyment. A person should declare that he has a poor memory only if he forgets many things that deeply interest him, and that he has made a sincere effort to remember.

It is an impossible task for us to remember things when we are concentrating on something else. If we are occupied with personal concerns, fears or even dreams, we cannot remember what others are saying to us or what we may be reading. We all have friends who were good students in college and who suddenly found themselves in love. Chances are that the experience left its rather permanent mark on the student in the form of lowered grades for the period.

Lack of Motivation

Another very important reason why people don't improve their memories is that they really see no very important reason for doing so. Nothing has motivated them to the point where they will take the extra effort and time to begin training themselves in better methods of memorizing. And since achieving a better memory is not merely a matter of acquiring the know-how of memory improvement techniques, but of constant practice as well, a person of little motivation may hear of the simple principles of memory improvement but will not spend the time drilling. In order to make memory improvement lasting, daily drilling is required.

False Assumptions

There is often an assumption that a good memory is a gift of God. That is only partially true. The gift that God has given each of us is the potential or the capacity to remember. Through proper training and effort, each person can improve his capacity for remembering up to the limits of that God-given potential. The sad, but true, fact is that very few of us come anywhere near our God-given capacity.

Confusion of Long Term and Short Term Memory

The confusion between long-term and short-term memory often causes a person to feel that there are only certain things that he can remember, such as telephone numbers because he has no trouble remembering many (home number, office number, parents' number, clients' numbers, etc.) while at the same time he feels that it is impossible to remember things like names, dates, scripture verses and so on. Much of this feeling can be eliminated once a person understands that we unconsciously decide many times a day whether we wish to remember something for just a short period of time, or whether we want to remember it for a long time. That unconscious selection then determines how we memorize.

For instance, most of the things that we need to

remember during a day we do not need to remember after that day is over so we do not *intend* to retain them. This intention—and remember, it's not a conscious process—causes us to forget things very quickly. The address of the shop we visited, directions to a motel in a strange city, the names of casual acquaintances met while traveling, the prices of various products that change from day to day, the combination of a lock in a locker room on a visit to the local YMCA. This is short-term memory.

In some cases we can actually cause ourselves to forget something that we remembered for several years, but now find unnecessary. How many of us can remember the telephone number (or maybe even the address) of the last home in which we lived? We may have lived there for several years, but since we do not intend to call or write that residence, we quickly forget those numbers when we leave.

On the other hand there are many things which we "intend" to remember for a long time, and so we do. We probably all remember our parents' telephone number. We may only call them two or three times a year, but we generally have no trouble remembering the number. Most books that we read we forget very quickly because we don't see their value for the future. A few books however are not just remembered but are actually outlined in our minds and we talk about them for years. Why? Because we perceive some value in them for the future, for ourselves, or for others.

Lack of Know How

There are many reasons for not improving our memories, but probably the biggest reason is that we never learned how. That's what this book is all about. In the following pages you will find out how you can dramatically strengthen your memory with little effort.

3
The Principles
of Memory
Improvement

NOW THAT WE KNOW what keeps people from having powerful memories, is there anything encouraging that can be said about principles of memory improvement as they apply to us? Yes, in fact, several principles for improvement are known that can be quickly learned by the very young as well as the old, and can be applied immediately.

PRINCIPLE #1

Memorize the General Thought

The foundation for all memory improvement programs is to memorize the general thought behind the thing that is to be recalled, and not to attempt word-for-word memorization. Rote memorization is remembering by sheer repetition, a going over and over the material until it is retained. With this method of memorizing, the material is easily lost, especially when we are under any kind of stress or pressure. Twenty-four hours after we have memorized by rote methods we will probably only remember a small portion of the information. It is much easier to attempt to remember the general thought of the information and then let that general thought be the device which reminds us of specific details. Not only are general ideas remembered much faster, but they are also retained much longer than the word-by-word method.

PRINCIPLE #2

Intend to Remember

We don't remember things we don't want to remember or don't intend to remember. Generally this is a good thing. It is estimated that a person deposits an average of ten thoughts every minute in his memory. This figures out to be approximately 300 million thoughts that enter our minds in a lifetime. It's a good thing that we forget or we would be overwhelmed by trivia. On the other hand, this means that we usually have a difficult time remembering things unless we make a conscious effort to remember them. Oh, there are certain things that we seem to have no trouble remembering, things such as the score of a crucial baseball game, the plot of a particularly good novel, or even the price paid for a favorite dress 3 years before. But this is different. In these cases no conscious attempt was made to remember, but the remembered things were of such high emotional interest for us that the intent to remember was present automatically. This natural interest level isn't automatically present for 95% of the things that are important for us to retain, so we must supply that intent. Fully intending to remember something, even stating that intent aloud will quite dramatically improve your memory.

PRINCIPLE #3

React Actively

There are two kinds of memory: Passive and Active. *Remembering* is passive memory. It is automatic. It is accomplished without effort and is usually triggered by association. Perhaps a name mentioned, a picture seen or a statement overheard will cause us to remember an old friend, or place, or even a tragic experience. *Recollection* on the other hand is active memory. In this case an attempt is purposely made to recall some person, fact, place or idea. Passive memory needs no training or help because it is automatic. Active memory needs methodical or systematized effort. This effort best takes five forms: repeating, writing and saying, grouping, reviewing, and using a memory system.

Repeat It

The more fully we react to what we want to remember, the better the chances that we will recall it when we need to. When we repeat (read, hear, say or write) the item to be remembered several times immediately, and then regularly over several days, the reaction is more likely to be adequate and long lasting. Remembering is always assisted by repetition, but when that repetition is spaced at regular intervals over several days rather than attempted all at once the retention is quite dramatic. In one study which compared the results of rereading technical material five times in one day with reading it once a day for five days, a month after reading, those who had reread it five times spread out over five days could recall nearly three times as much as the others who had reread it five times in one day.

Repetition is a simple technique for more efficient remembering.

Write It Down—Say It Aloud

Another way to react actively is to write down whatever it is that you wish to remember. Even the brainiest person forgets more than he remembers, and about one-half of what he believes he remembers is inaccurate at least in part. Writing things down is important. This has the obvious benefit of giving you a record for further referral somewhere in the future (that is if you can remember where you put your notes) but also of forcing you to review and concentrate much more intensively on what it is that you intend to remember. When you write it down you not only think the thought one time very rapidly before you write, but you again think the thought as you write—only this time much more slowly. This word-by-word thinking and writing requires a mental and physical coordination which has a cementing effect on the material to be remembered. Most of the world's achievers have made steady use of this principle. They are always carrying around note pads or 3 × 5 cards and jotting things down. Some of us neglect to write things down because we feel it will strengthen our memories if we depend on memory alone. This is nonsense.

Another way to help remember things is to talk to yourself so that you can clearly hear what you are saying. If we will repeat aloud what it is that we would like to remember, we will generally remember between 30% and 40% more.

If we are reading and want to remember what we are reading, we can efficiently combine talking and reading to do so. The most efficient way to do this is to first read silently and rapidly to get the overview of the material. Then from time to time pause to recite the gist of what has been read in the last few minutes and pages. When reading and reciting are combined in this manner most people will easily find that they can remember 3 to 4 times as much and for a longer period of time.

Many successful Christian leaders and executives wind up all their meetings and interviews by briefly summarizing to the other persons the matters that have been discussed and the decisions that have been made. This not only brushes up the memory, clarifies, and reinforces what has been said, but it also makes it certain that there are no misunderstandings or false conclusions.

Group Things Together

We also remember things easier by combining the things to be memorized into patterns or groups. This is especially true for lists or numbers.

The average adult can fairly easily remember a span of 7 or 8 numbers. It is possible occasionally for a person to exert considerable effort and stretch himself so as to handle slightly longer numbers. This is called memory stretching. Thus the man with the natural span of 8 numerals can occasionally remember 10 with special effort. But this stretching does have its limits. When a person stretches too much, something snaps. If the man with the natural span of 8 tries to remember 11 numerals, he often finds that his memory shrinks to 5 or 6. However, if this same person divides the numbers into two groups of 6, he very often can remember a span of 12 numerals. Usually the sermons that are easiest to remember probably have the key thoughts grouped around a few points that go together.

A rule can come out of this. Whenever you have long lists to remember, group them in smaller units which naturally seem to fit together.

Review Regularly

Since forgetting sets in within a few seconds after anything is learned, another secret of a good memory is to review on a regular basis. It is especially important to keep material fresh in our minds for the first several days. Several significant studies have shown that most adults will forget 2/3 of everything they read within 24 hours and about 90% within a week. Forgetting of any information is enormous within the first few days, almost as bad within the first two weeks, but slows down after that. Therefore anything you can retain for the first two weeks has every chance of staying with you permanently, especially if you review the material during the first several days and follow the additional suggestions coming up in the next section of this book.

Some information does not have to be brushed up very often in order to have it become permanent. Anything that strikes us as especially significant or important has a tendency to stick with us much easier. Things that make sense to us or that seem to have immediate application don't need to be brushed up as often to make them permanent.

In short, anything we think important, refer to often, or brush up occasionally, seldom leaves us.

4
Use a Memory System

PRINCIPLE #4

THE FIRST THREE principles that we've discussed so far (Can you remember them? 1. Memorize the general thought. 2. Intend to remember. 3. React actively by repeating, writing it and saying it aloud, grouping things together and reviewing regularly. Review them!) have been principles equally applicable to general memory improvement of all types. Adoption of these principles will result in an increased ability to retain information. This chapter discusses the 4th principle. This 4th principle may be almost as important as the other three principles put together, and what's more it is immediately applicable for both specific and general memory problems of all types. This principle can be simply stated, "Learn and use a memory system."

A memory system is simply an organized approach to memorizing anything, and generally results in ease of memorizing and a much higher retention rate. The same person who earlier memorized by simple repetition and retained only 20%, can raise that to an 80 or 90% retention by following the memory improvement techniques that follow. Through their use, material is easy to memorize, is recalled with little effort, and is generally immune to mixing and interference from other materials, even under stress.

There are six different memory systems that will be helpful in memorizing data:

The Rhyme System:

The Acrostic System:

The Translation System:

The Imagination and Exaggeration System:

The Stacking and Yoking System:

The Position System:

Each of these systems will be briefly explained and then their specific applications will be discussed in the following chapters. In order to develop a powerful memory for yourself, you must adopt a specific system of memory or a combination of systems and then follow it.

1. *The Rhyme System*

Nearly all memory systems were invented before the invention of printing, and many before the invention of writing. Chants and crude verse were often employed by religious leaders to assist their people in remembering theological truths, dogma, or religious responses. Educators have been using rhymes for years to assist children in remembering. Nearly all of us still rely on

> Thirty days hath September,
> April, June, and November.
> All the rest have thirty one,
> Once short February's done.

There are numerous rhymes to help us with our spelling problems. For those of us who can't remember whether to use "ie," or "ei" in spelling, the following rhyme has been used often:

> I before E
> Except after C
> Or when sounded like A,
> As in neighbor or weigh.

Although the device of putting material to be remembered into verse is not promoted as much now as it has been in past years it is still useful. If you have any facility for "versifying," you may find it easy and entertaining to make up your own rhymes, such as:

> By calling DO 2-6286, I can,
> Speak immediately with JoAnn.

Or if you are to pick up some things at the grocery store, you might create a rhyme like this:

> Tomatoes, carrots, meat, and spices a few,
> Will help young Betty to make a stew.

Although this is poor rhyme and certainly worse poetry, these catchy (and often funny) rhymes are easily created and are a definite aid to memory.

2. The Acrostic System

The word acrostic means, a composition, usually in verse, in which the first or last letters of the lines, or other letters, taken in order, form a motto, phrase, name or word. Most of us have used, at one time or another, the first letter of each thing to be memorized to form another word or series of words. The letters of that word then reminded us of the things to be remembered. There are many acrostics that have become a part of our everyday language. For example, the word *snafu,* from the military, is an acrostic for "situation normal, all fouled up!" The acrostic that would be formed if you were trying to remember a shopping list containing the items sugar, margarine, steak, bread, ice cream, eggs, apples, flour, milk, oysters, might be *smsbie afmo;* or if you wanted to rearrange the items a bit you could create an acrostic that reads, *Beaf Is Moms.* As you can see, this phrase would be easily remembered, and in turn, each letter would serve as a reminder of the item to be remembered.

This system of acrostics is especially effective when there are long lists of unrelated items to be remembered, but may also be used for remembering a series of scripture verses, phrases or ideas.

If you have a series of ideas to be remembered, the ideas must first be boiled down to a key word or phrase so that the first letter of the verse, key word or phrase may be identified. For example, you may want to remember the following ideas and verses of scripture, and in the order given.

Man's Need
All have sinned. Rom. 3:23
The results of sin. Rom. 6:23

Man's Response
We can't save ourselves. Eph. 2:8-9
Repentance is important. Acts 17:30
Believing is important. Acts 16:30-31

God's Remedy
He loves the world. Jn. 3:16-17
He proved his love for us. Rom. 5:8

The first step is to note that there are three parts to this list of ideas: The first part has two ideas, the second has three ideas, the third has two. You might select the words *Need, Response, Remedy* as your summary words for these three parts of the list.

Under *Need,* the first idea might be summarized by the word *all,* and the second idea might be summarized by the key word *results.* The acrostic formed for this first part of the list is *Nar.* The N is capitalized to remind you that it is the division summary word.

Under *Response* the first idea may be summarized by the word *ourselves,* the second idea by the word *repentance,* and the third by the word *believing.* The acrostic formed for this second part is *Rorb.*

Under *Remedy* the first idea may be summarized with the word *loves,* and the second idea with the word *proved.* The acrostic formed for the last part is *Rlp.*

Now that we have boiled down all of the ideas to key summary words and have formed words from the first letters of these words we can use the acrostic "sentence" formed to easily remember the ideas and their verses. Now the sentence "Nar Rorb Rlp" is rather funny to look at but it is an effective mnemonic device. Try it now.

Can you remember what the three division words are that are indicated by the capital letters? What ideas do these summary words remind you of? Now can you remember the other ideas represented by the rest of the letters?

Remembering the ideas in the correct order, or the order presented, is a simple matter of keeping the letters of the acrostic in the same order as the ideas. Sometimes, however, the order is not important. In that case you may want to rearrange some or all of the letters to form other words easier to remember. For instance the acrostic we just formed could be rearranged to read raN Rorb Rpl (pronounced, ran roarb ripple). It's a little easier to say.

The acrostic is one of the easiest of all memory methods to employ immediately and has application for a great many tasks.

3. The Translation System

Numerous studies have shown that it is much easier to remember words than to remember numbers. Unfortunately, however, we live in an age when the need to use and remember numbers is growing. A traveler abroad often must write out his passport number two or three times a day. Social security numbers, driver's license numbers, banking and checking account numbers, credit card numbers and student identification numbers are just a few of the identifying numbers that each of us have. Home addresses, telephone numbers, office and client addresses, dates, price information, and many other numbers which change occasionally must be remembered constantly. This often gets to be a problem.

Sometimes when I travel I will stay in a different hotel every night. After about 10 days of staying in a different room every night and consequently having different room numbers, I have a difficult time remembering which room I'm in unless I make some effort to concentrate on each day's new room number. Occasionally I have attempted to enter the wrong room because it had the number of the room of the motel I was in the evening before! That has proved embarrassing. Even more often I have eaten a meal in the motel restaurant and almost signed the wrong room number to the bill. Yes, numbers are important, but difficult to remember for any length of time unless a memory system is employed.

For hundreds of years people who have been successful in remembering numbers have been doing so because they *have* been using a memory system which translates numbers into easily remembered words. This translation system is easily learned and permits ease of remembering. Here's how it works.

Numerals are abstract digits, with very little meaning and hard to remember. If we use a system to convert these numbers to easily recognized words which have meaning and then remember these words which stand for numbers we will find memorizing numbers much easier. These picture words are the key. Let me illustrate: If I want to remember my social security number, 319-89-3472, and with little effort, I think of "Balloon Can Burst!" The letters of these words stand for 319-89-3472 according to a translation system which converts numbers to letters so that easily remembered words are what are remembered rather than the more difficult to remember numbers.

It works like this. For each number from 0 through 9 a letter or combination of letters is designated. This system disregards vowels and operates on the basis of *how words sound*, rather than how they should be correctly spelled.

Memory Aid

0 = d	d without the stem is a zero
1 = l	l is one stroke
2 = T	T is two strokes
3 = B	B is three strokes
4 = M,R	M is four strokes, r is the last letter in four
5 = F	F is the first letter in the word five
6 = G	a capital G looks like a six
7 = S	S is the first letter in seven
8 = K	An 8 is a K with curves on top and bottom
9 = N	N is the first letter in nine

A person can very quickly memorize the letter designations for each of the ten numbers. When this happens any number can quickly be converted to a series of letters. Thus, my social security number, 319-89-3472, is seen as B1N-KN-BRST.

Pause at this point for a few moments and memorize the letter designations and their number equivalents by writing them down several times. While doing this also review the memory aid for each one.

The next step is to make words out of the letter combinations by adding vowel sounds where appropriate. When you do this, don't worry about proper spelling. Just stress how it sounds. The combination of letters becomes "Balloon Can Burst." This phrase is easier to remember than the numbers were. And since this is the case, later on when you wish to remember the number you simply translate the consonant sounds (not vowel sounds) back into numbers.

Any word can have a number equivalent.

Word		Consonant sounds		Number equivalent
dog	=	dg	=	06
mouse	=	ms	=	47
factory	=	fktre	=	5824
antihistamine	=	Ntstmn	=	927249

4. The Imagination and Exaggeration System

The ability to imagine easily is of considerable help when it comes to the role of exaggeration in memory improvement. It is a well established fact that the things which we can visually imagine and then exaggerate out of proportion are easily remembered and for long periods of time.

If one wishes to remember one thing or a series of things this is how imagination and exaggeration might work. If the thing you need to remember is to stop at the florist and pick up a flower arrangement you might imagine your car as jammed completely full of flowers with them sticking out of every available opening: flowers coming out from under the hood; from out of the windows and under the bumpers. Using your imagination you might even imagine a satin ribbon tied around the car with the words "Rest In Peace" printed on it. You might even imagine a gigantic card stuck in the car door with the name of the giver on it, or the florist where you have to pick up the arrangement.

If you have a series of things to remember, such as a grocery list containing the following items, you should use imagination and exaggeration just as effectively.

eggs	apples
ham	cheese
toothpaste	carrots
paperbags	tomato soup
milk	bar of soap

To remember eggs you might imagine a gigantic egg of an ostrich, perhaps frying in a small pan.

Next picture several small hams sprinkled over the frying egg.

Then imagine a gigantic tube of toothpaste that has been squeezed in the middle and is shooting out toothpaste lying across the frying pan.

The toothpaste which is being squeezed out is falling into, and quickly filling, a paperbag.

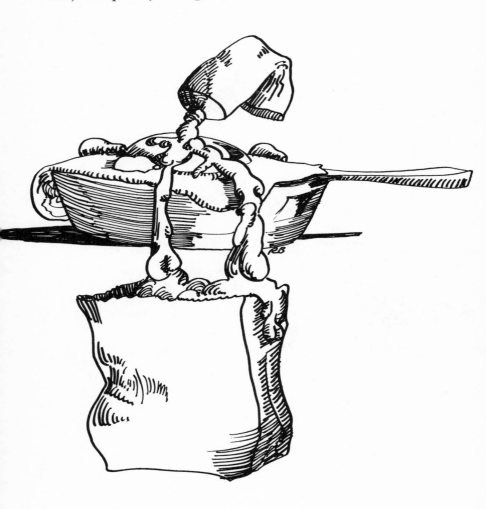

The paperbag as it fills tips and knocks over a glass of milk. The milk comes pouring out quickly and floods the floor.

Soon, the only thing visible are apples, cut in half with the core taken out so that they float around looking like small row boats.

After a few moments you climb on top of your tomato soup can. Now, because it is Saturday night you decide to take a bath. Reaching into your pocket you pull out a bar of soap and begin lathering up. In fact, you get so sudsy that you are simply a mass of soap bubbles.

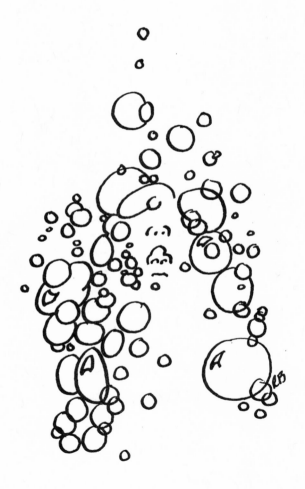

Now, at first, this imaginative exercise in exaggeration may appear childish, but I would guess that nearly all of us now, and after just one reading of the above sentences and a quick look at each of the pictures, remember the ten items we are to get from the store. Don't we? Run through them in your mind. As you begin with your first item you will find it rather easy to picture with the mind's eye, each item.

If we had given the same amount of time it has taken us to read through the above paragraphs to attempting to memorize the list by rote memory, most of us would probably have difficulty remembering six or seven of the ten items.

Imagination and exaggeration are important memory tools. This use of visualized imagination and exaggeration to assist in remembering has been used by mankind for thousands of years. The primitive cave paintings of hunting scenes and the growing of crops were attempts to use visual reminders, often exaggerated, of important events. The Egyptian system of hieroglyphics carved in ancient tombs and the pyramids show that the early Egyptians recognized the value of the visual portrayal of events and customs. One does not even have to be able to read ancient Egyptian to be able to reconstruct some of the meanings in the ancient writings. The pictures tell the story by suggesting the event or custom being written about.

Some of the best examples for us of the use of imagination and exaggeration in causing us to remember are found in the teachings of Christ. He was constantly communicating difficult to understand ideas to his disciples through the use of parables and imaginative illustrations. When he declared, "I am the door," "Behold, I stand at the door, and knock," "I am the good shepherd," "In my Father's house are many mansions," he did not intend for his disciples or for us to think that he was a literal door, or that he was actually knocking on one, or that he was really a shepherd, or that somewhere he had a whole neighborhood of houses for us to physically live in. And the disciples did not for an instant think these things. They, like us, immediately saw Christ's statements, his parables, as imaginative visualizations of the truth he wished us to know. In an instant, through this exaggeration, he communicated ideas and truths that it takes us hundreds of pages in theology books to adequately explain. Through the use of these visualizations we are quickly and clearly reminded of the truth God would have us learn and remember.

And we do remember. Most of us would be hard pressed to remember the teachings of Christ without first remembering the parables. In fact, even the cross has become the visual reminder of the great doctrine of salvation. Not one of us can look at the cross symbol without it reminding us of the meaning of the cross.

Exaggeration and imagination are important in remembering. We use the easily remembered and visualized object to remind us of the harder to remember teaching, idea, list, place or any number of things.

5. *The Stacking and Yoking System*

Another crucial concept in improved memory training for the Christian worker is the idea of yoking and stacking. Yoking simply means that where there are several things to remember, each item should *touch* the next item. This physical touching is necessary so that in our mind's eye we can look at one item and see where it touches the next item. This way each item leads to the next item which in turn leads to the next. The actual touching enables us to be led from one item to the next.

If you attempt to remember what a long lost friend or relative looks like you normally find it difficult to do so unless you attempt to reconstruct his appearance part by part. For instance, you might first attempt to visualize the person's hair. With some effort you generally can do this. Then letting your mental eyes gaze over the hairdo you are led to the forehead. Visualizing the forehead you are led to the eyebrows and eyes. Traveling further down the face you touch the nose and perhaps the cheekbone and cheeks. Still visualizing you are led from the nose and cheeks to the lips, teeth and mouth. You then proceed to the chin and throat and ultimately the complete body. Since each part leads to the next you are simply letting the known part lead you to remember the next element, and then the next and so on. Try visualizing a friend's face and see if I'm not right about one part touching the next and acting as a path to follow in your visualization. Remember, the things you wish to remember must touch in at least one spot.

Stacking is similar to yoking in that it is easier to remember a series of things or concepts if they are touching by being piled up one on top of the other. This is generally much more dramatic for us and easier to visualize and remember than when things are "normally" lined up side by side as if they were spread out on a table.

This stacking also makes it easy to yoke items in dramatic ways. The ideas, represented by concrete images (salvation, for instance, may be represented by the visual symbol of the cross), or things can be piled in dramatic ways and can be yoked by the places where they touch.

The following list of 10 things can illustrate the concepts of yoking and stacking as well as the value of imagination and exaggeration.

1. Tower	6. Tree
2. Watermelon	7. Airplane
3. Clock	8. Hook
4. Spear	9. Book
5. Monkey	10. Car

As you read through the next few paragraphs attempt to do several things: 1. Use your imagination to see in your mind's eye the exaggerated appearances suggested for the list of 10 items to be remembered. 2. Consciously attempt to *stack* the items one upon the other as you visualize them. Sometimes closing your eyes helps in the visualizing process. 3. Make certain that you *yoke* each object to the preceding item in the list. Glance occasionally at the pictures of the items in the book to see where each item actually touches. 4. Remember that the ability to remember a list like this is always less the first time you try. Memorizing gets easier each time you use the methods suggested here, so keep working at it. You'll be surprised at how easily you memorize in the future.

The first item on the list is *tower,* so let's visualize a specific tower, one that is well known to us—the Eiffel Tower. But let's exaggerate and distort it in some manner so that it is memorable. Since the Eiffel Tower is large, let's imagine it small. In fact, how about two feet tall? Do you see it in your mind as well as on the page? Good.

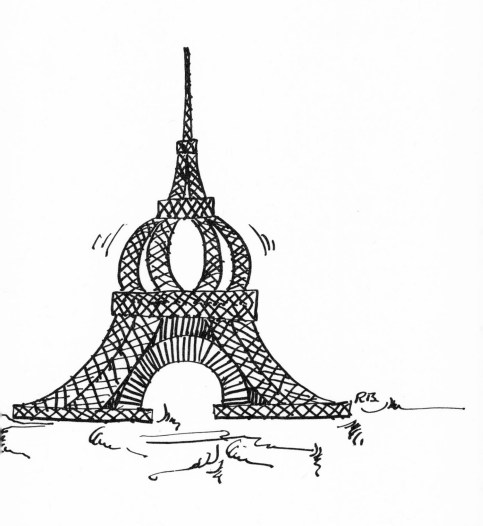

The second item is *watermelon*. How do you imagine a watermelon? Right! Cut in half with all that sweet pink goodness ready to be eaten. That's not hard to imagine at all. But now let's stack it. Mentally lift that piece of watermelon and jam it down on top of the tower so that the tower point impales the watermelon and holds it in place. Not only is it now stacked, it is yoked. Now, as you visualize the tower and your mind's eye travels up the tower you are naturally led to the point where the watermelon is yoked.

The third item to be remembered is *clock*. Let's imagine a schoolroom clock but let's distort it by grabbing the minute hand and pulling it straight down so that the hand is stretched so long it hangs down beyond the clock face. Now let's stack and yoke. Since each object needs to be yoked to the preceding one, our clock must touch the watermelon. Well then, stand the clock on top of the watermelon by stabbing the long minute hand into the watermelon.

Next comes *spear.* This one's easy. Since our rules say that we must touch the preceding object, our spear must touch the clock. But, where? Let's take the spear and shove it right through the center of the clock. Now we have a clock with a long spear through it.

The next item on the list is *monkey*. What shall we have him yoked to? That's right, the spear. Picture the monkey sitting on the spear. The stack is getting taller, but notice how much easier it is getting to imagine these things.

We now have five items in our stack. Starting with tower, review the 5 objects by visualizing them one at a time. Make certain that you visually note where each item yokes to the next. If there isn't a good clear yoke you will have a difficult time being led from one thing to the next.

The sixth item is *tree.* Let's imagine a specific kind of tree. How about a gigantic redwood. And since we have to yoke tree to monkey let's have the monkey holding the tree up in the air with one hand. Now that takes imagination!

Item number seven is *airplane.* This is another easy one. Let's have the airplane crash (but gently!) into the top of the redwood tree. After all, that tree is sticking up in the air so high that you might expect a plane to hit it.

The eighth thing on our list is *hook*. That's a little more difficult to visualize. But if we use our imagination freely we won't have much trouble. When I think of hook I immediately think of a fishhook, so I'm going to imagine a gigantic fishhook and I'm going to hook it through the tail of the airplane.

Next we have *book*. A good way to stack and yoke the book is to first visualize a paperback book rolled into a tube and shoved through the eye of the fishhook.

The last item on the list is *car*. If I'm going to use my imagination to picture a car I'm going to visualize the best. Picture a Rolls-Royce that costs thirty or forty thousand dollars. Now we must yoke it to the book. Using the principle of exaggeration let's shrink the Rolls-Royce to the size of a toy car and then let's drive the car through the book (which is in the shape of a tube) and out the other end! Poor car!

That does it. We've finished visualizing, stacking and yoking our list of ten unrelated items. Can you say them in order? I'm certain you can. But to prove to yourself how effective this method is, try the following experiment. Repeat the list in order again, but this time do it *backwards*. Start with the tenth item and work backwards to number one. As soon as you try this you will discover that it doesn't matter if you go backwards or forwards, you will remember the list equally well either way!

As long as you keep stacking and yoking, each thing to be remembered will lead you easily to the next item.

6. The Position System

Do # 1-50

We also need an easy method for determining a position in any long list of items. For instance, it would be nice to be able to instantly recall things such as which book of the Bible is the 37th book, or remember what's on page 17 of a specific magazine, or even what the 44th state was that was admitted to the Union. This ability can be learned, and very quickly. All that is necessary is that we memorize specific visual objects or concrete reminders for each number, say up to 500, and then yoke the item to be memorized with that visual image for the number.

Now don't panic when I say you need to remember 500 objects. It's really not bad. In fact, it's very easy. Since the same visual image will always be used with a specific number, and will never be used for anything else, and since these visual images are easily remembered because they *rhyme* with the number they represent, to memorize 500 position numbers will not be too difficult.

Actually, we only need to remember 32 images to create 500 positions. We will remember images for the numbers from 1 through 19, and for numbers 20, 30, 40, 50, 60, 70, 80, 90, 100, 200, 300, 400, 500.

Knowing these 32 numbers will be all that is necessary for creating any number up to 500. First memorize the 32 numbers below and their visual images, and then we'll learn how they are used to remember position or place. As you read the number, repeat it aloud along with the rhyme word. This way you quickly learn to associate the number, the sound of the rhyme word, and its visual image.

1—GUN

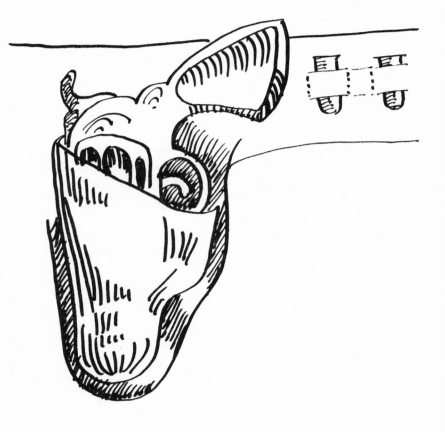

4—MOWER

5—DIVE

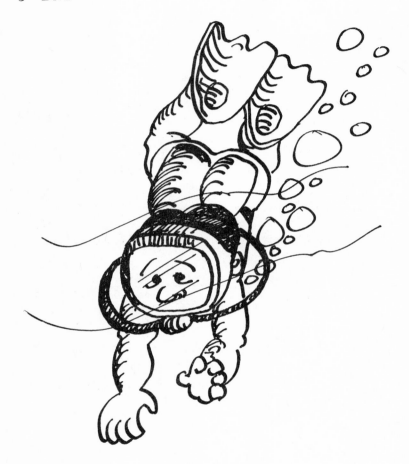

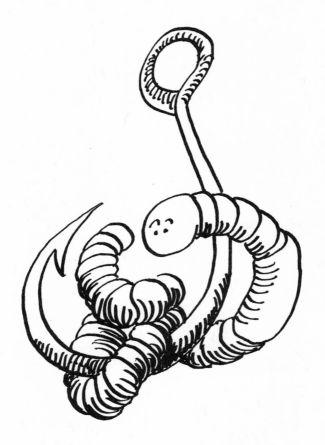

9—MINE

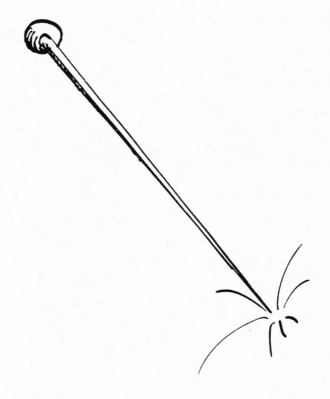

30—DIRTY

Go over this list four or five times so that the list is easily recalled before you go any further.

Now that you have committed 32 numbers and their visual images to memory here is how you use these 32 numbers to create actually 599 positions. To indicate a number in the twenties such as 22, you simply use the descriptive adjective for twenty and add the visual image for two so that twenty-two is represented by minty-moo, a peppermint striped cow.

Twenty-three is minty-free, a peppermint striped bird flying free.

Thirty-one is dirty-gun.

Thirty-two is dirty-moo, and so on.

One hundred twenty-two is a minty-moo in the rain.

Three hundred seventy-one is a gun with a halo over it in the fog.

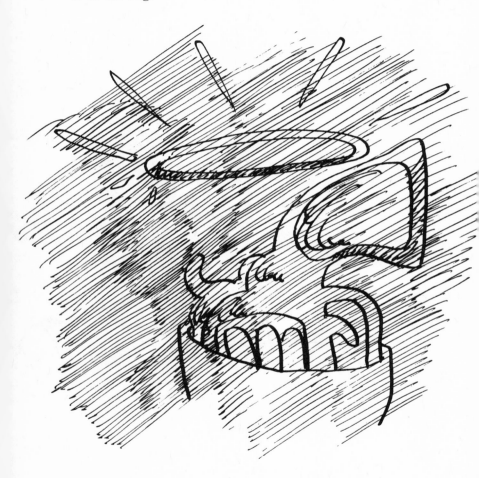

As you can see, these 32 images can be combined in a number of ways so as to enable you to create 599 position numbers. Once you have learned these position numbers and their images it is a simple matter to yoke the item to be remembered to the position number. It works like this:

Perhaps you have occasion to remember a list of 25 items in order, and you need to be able to determine quickly which item is number 13, or 22, or 7. As you begin to memorize your list, simply create a visual image for each item and then yoke it to the number image that you have just learned. If number 13 on your list is a casserole, use your imagination to visualize a casserole, perhaps of gigantic proportions. Next think of the number 13. The rhyme word image for number 13 is flirting and you quickly see the winking eyes as the image. Now yoke the two images together. One way to do this is to imagine the casserole shoved into the winking eye.

In the future to remember what is yoked to number 13, you quickly repeat the number 13, remember its rhyming image of the flirting eyes and then using your mind's eye see what item is shoved into the winking eye. In this case it's a casserole.

You would do the same thing for each of the items on your list. This way you very quickly create a method for remembering the position of up to 599 items or ideas.

What about memorizing the position of the books of the Bible? After you have learned your images for the 500 positions, the next thing you need to do is to make certain that you have determined a visual image for each Bible book name. For instance, the fourth book of the Bible is Deuteronomy, and its visual image could easily be two law books piled on top of one another, because the word Deuteronomy means the second giving of the law. Since the number 4 has as its rhyme word Mower, and is represented by a lawn mower, yoke your law books to the mower by visually imagining that you are shoving the books into the mower blades. Make certain that the mower and the books actually yoke so that you can travel in your mind's eye from one image to the next.

This way at a later date when you want to remember what the fourth book of the Bible is, you simply think of the sound-alike image for the number 4, which is mower, and then in your mind's eye look to see what the mower is cutting up. Yoked to the mower and getting chopped up in the blades are two law books. You quickly remember that the two law books represent Deuteronomy. Hence the fourth book of the Bible is Deuteronomy. You can do this quickly for every book of the Bible.

Remember, the rhyming position images you yoke to are always the same for their numbers. Since you will never use those images of the gun, cow (moo), bird (free), mower and so on for anything except the position numbers, you will very quickly develop almost instantaneous ability to establish and remember the position of things and ideas.

5
Memorizing
Scripture

WHILE IN AFRICA recently I had occasion to speak to a large group of National Christian leaders on the subject, Scripture Memorization Techniques. Because of my conservative theological background in the States, I just assumed that all Christians in the world placed the same high priority on scripture memorization as a part of the Christian life that I did. But I was wrong. As I spoke of the ease with which my listeners would be able to memorize scripture after listening to me and then applying the memorization techniques, I was interrupted by an African pastor with a question.

"Brother Johnson, why should we memorize scripture? Wouldn't our time be better spent on visitation, studying, or reading the Bible?"

My reaction to that question at first was one of confusion. Was this man suggesting that scripture memorization by any method was wasted time? When I asked for clarification, the pastor quickly made clear that of all

131

the important things he needed to be concerned with in the ministry, memorizing scripture had to be at the bottom of his list of priorities. It became obvious that there were three reasons for this attitude.

"Memorizing scripture is a chore with little practical benefit because of the difficulty I have in memorizing. But not only does it take a great amount of work and time but I forget the verses so quickly. What's the use of memorizing scripture if I forget it within a few days? But also, many of the verses suggested in the scripture memory programs I've tried have very little meaning for me. If I don't really understand them and they don't really have any application for me at the moment, I don't see how I can benefit from them. As a result I forget them very fast."

Scripture Is Hard to Memorize, Easily Forgotten, and Often Without Meaning

This pastor quickly and practically identified the three major hindrances to scripture memorization wherever it is tried. Christian men and women in Chicago, London, Tokyo, all over the world have been saying that it is good to memorize scripture, but it is too hard to enjoy doing, the verses are forgotten so quickly that memorizing seems pointless, and they don't really know which verses or portions to memorize.

But don't despair. There is a way to memorize scripture that uses what you have learned so far in this memory book and actually makes the act of memorizing an enjoyable experience. Using tested memory techniques, scripture memorizing becomes much easier than it has ever been before; the verses you memorize will not be easily forgotten; and the process of memorizing will actually force you to concentrate on the meaning of the verses so that they are never abstract or divorced from personal application to your life.

Crucial Questions

Before we actually begin the process of memorizing, there are three bothersome questions that need to be dealt with.

1. Which version of the Bible should we memorize?
2. Should we memorize a passage word for word, or should we memorize thoughts?
3. Is there a system for selecting verses to memorize that will give direction and organization to our memorization, or should we just obtain a packet of memory verses and memorize them in the order suggested?

Which Version?

Which version of the Bible you select as your memorization version should depend on your purpose in memorizing. In fact, you may want to memorize scripture passages from several different versions. For instance: There are many passages of scripture that you will want to commit to memory for their contemplation and meditation value. They are "thought" verses and your purpose is to dwell on them in moments of meditation and quietness. Therefore, you may want to consider memorizing them from a modern translation such as *The Living Bible*. *The Living Bible's* everyday vocabulary and phrasing lends itself well to this kind of scripture meditation.

On the other hand, if you are memorizing scripture primarily for use in a public ministry, perhaps for quoting to a congregation while delivering a sermon, your memorizing purpose is different and this purpose should guide you in your version choice. Under these "public" memorization purposes you probably should select the version of the Bible that most of your listeners are most familiar with. This may be the commonly used King James Version. Quotations from the version familiar to your listeners will strike responsive chords in memories. Thus, you will give your listeners a sense of familiarity and confidence in what you are saying, and they in turn will tend to listen better. In short: pick your purpose, then pick your version.

Word for Word?

For scores of years scripture memorization advocates have stressed memorizing Bible verses word for word. Every little *a, and,* or *the* needed to be in its correct spot. An ending left off a word, or an *and* left out of a verse could be the death knell for the competitor in the Annual Sunday School Memorization Contest, and might even keep the competitor from winning the free week at summer camp!

The two main reasons for the development of this heavy emphasis on word-by-word memorization are tradition and the lack of alternate versions in past generations.

For thousands of years it was important for us to memorize scripture word for word because in large measure that was how scripture was passed along from one generation to the next. Thus accuracy was vital. Before we had easily accessible or available copies of the Bible, we had to carefully quote it to one another and thus preserve it orally. Extraordinarily fortunate was the man two or three hundred years ago who was able to read passages of scripture to his family and friends. Only the well educated and relatively affluent families owned Bibles. Now, even though the Bible in its many versions is the most commonly available book in the world, we still hang on to the tradition which suggests that "for the sake of accuracy in preserving the Word of God, memorize scripture word by word."

Also, when there were just one or two commonly read versions of the Bible anyway, there was no reason not to memorize scripture word for word. Now, however, there are literally dozens of commonly used versions all saying the same thing but with slightly different selections of words. It quickly becomes obvious to most of us that there is no special blessing from God that comes with certain words being learned in a certain order. The blessing of the scripture and of the Holy Spirit comes when the meaning of the words is understood, when God's thoughts become clear to our minds and hearts. This usually does not require memorizing every single word in a verse, but instead needs only memorizing of the things necessary for correct meaning and order of ideas.

Having said all of this, let me add one more item. One of the best ways to memorize scripture is to memorize it word for word. It is orderly and logical and provides a sense of completeness to the memorizing process. Memorize word for word if you feel this fits your memorizing needs and personality. The important thing is to memorize!

Which Verse?

One of the problems with trying to memorize scripture

is the problem of determining a reasonable assortment of scripture passages to commit to memory. Haphazard, pick and choose methods of memorizing scripture do work, but are certainly not desirable. The Christian worker ought to memorize according to some plan so that he brings purpose and direction to his memorizing. This does not mean that he should simply obtain a list of scripture memory cards and begin memorizing them in the order suggested. This order of memorization is the order that had meaning for the person who established the order. Those same verses may not have the same relevance for you. This predetermined order would be all right, but there is a better way to memorize so that the verses selected are important to you and as a result are not as easily forgotten. This selection method also ties in with effective Bible study.

I suggest that every time you read a passage from the Bible, that you pause after you finish reading and briefly try to summarize the most important idea, admonition, or truth that the passage seems to be presenting. Most scripture portions contain more than one significant idea or truth, but try to isolate what *you* feel is the main idea. After you have decided what the main thought of the passage is go back over the passage and attempt to find the one verse which best summarizes or identifies that main thought. That verse then becomes the verse to memorize.

Using this method you will quickly develop the habit of reviewing the passages you read and contemplating the truths contained. This by itself is helpful. But this also provides an opportunity for the Holy Spirit to speak to our hearts.

The Work of the Holy Spirit

We all believe that the Holy Spirit speaks to our hearts and minds. But when does this happen? Perhaps it happens when we rush rapidly through a passage and then close the Bible and rush off to job or school. More likely, the Holy Spirit speaks to us when we quietly and calmly *contemplate* what we have read. If we are *looking* for what is important in what we read, the Holy Spirit will honor that intent and direct us. We are much less likely to fall into error in our Bible reading this way.

You will also find that this method of selecting scripture enables you to develop an excellent grasp of the content of the Bible. Eventually, you will be able to identify the subject of almost any chapter or major portion in a matter of seconds. For instance, if you read John chapter 3 and then contemplate its contents, you will probably identify the main idea of John 3 as Salvation through Jesus Christ. If you then reread the chapter looking for the verse which best captures that idea you will probably select verse 16. Thus John 3:16 becomes your memory verse and the reminder of the subject of chapter three.

After you have memorized the verse, you will find you have some extra benefits. Becuase of the way you selected the verse, you now know where to find a chapter on Salvation if necessary. Then someday when you may seek a passage on Salvation, all you have to do is recall your salvation verse and its reference to know that John 3 is the passage to read. In like manner, sometime in the future you may want to know what chapter 3 of John is about, all you have to do is recall your key verse from John 3, repeat it to yourself and you can quickly see that since it has salvation as its subject, John 3 must also have salvation as its central subject.

In short, use your memory verse as an aid in understanding and recalling the organization and ideas in the Bible.

Everything we have said about memory training to this point will be useful in memorizing scripture, but there are three major memory concepts that will be stressed: exaggeration, stacking and yoking.

Let's Memorize Scripture

Let's take a scripture verse and try to memorize it using these three key memory improvement elements.

The scripture verse we are going to memorize is I Corinthians 12:28. This verse says, "And God hath set some in the church, first apostles, secondarily prophets, thirdly teachers, after that miracles, then gifts of healing, helps, governments, diversities of tongues."

Using our three basic memory techniques—exaggeration, stacking and yoking—we're going to memorize this verse according to a pattern that you should use for memorizing all scripture verses. Obviously it will take you less time to memorize future verses because you will be applying the techniques in your own mind and not reading. This verse will provide the model for future memorizing.

"And God hath set some in the church . . ."

First imagine a large hand reaching down from the clouds (the hand from the clouds suggests God). The hand is holding a chair. This is not just an ordinary chair, but a pulpit chair, the kind you see at the front of the church in which the preacher sits on Sunday morning. The heavenly hand sets the chair in the front door of a very small New England type church ("And God hath set some in the church . . .").

"first apostles . . ."

As the hand sets the chair in the front doorway of
the church, we see walking up the steps toward the chair
a figure in long white robes. This figure is an apostle
("first apostles"). We know he is an apostle because he
looks like our picture of a dignified apostle: he has long
hair, a long beard, long white flowing robes. As he sits
down in the chair, we know for certain he is an apostle
because on his chest, like a gigantic high school letter,
is the letter "A". You guessed it—the "A" stands for
apostle.

"secondarily prophets . . ."

As we watch, the apostle looks back down toward the front steps and sees a second person walking up the steps and reaching out to shake hands with him. This is the prophet ("secondarily prophets"). How do we know he is a prophet? Because he looks like a prophet. He also wears a long robe, but his robe is worn looking. It looks like burlap. His hair is all tangled and his beard unkempt. It appears that he has been wandering in the desert or wilderness for a long time. He has the aroma of the desert. He looks like John the Baptist would look if John had been out in the wilderness a long time. Now how do we know for certain that he is a prophet? Look carefully. We can see he is a prophet because as he turns around we can see his chest. On his chest is a large . . . "P"? Wrong! On his chest is a large dollar sign! Why a dollar sign? Because a dollar sign stands for prophet (profit). Certainly, it's the wrong word for prophet, but the exaggeration involved in relating the profit sign to our prophet will be good for our memory.

"thirdly teachers . . ."

Next we see seated on the prophet's shoulder a small
figure. As we get closer and look at him we see he is
a teacher ("thirdly teachers"). How do we know he is
a teacher? Again because of the way he is dressed! He
is wearing long academic robes, he has a graduation cap
perched on his head, and the graduation tassle hangs
over one eye. Under one arm he is even carrying a stack
of books.

Notice how we are stacking the characters and how they are all yoking? Review the visual images as you review the first part of the verse. "God hath set some in the church, first apostles, secondarily prophets, thirdly teachers."

"after that miracles . . ."

Now as we run our mind's eye over the teacher we see him holding in one hand a large silver goblet. This is the kind of goblet that looks rather like an old fashioned communion cup. As we look inside that cup we see it is holding water which is in the process of turning to wine. This stands for miracles ("after that miracles"). The marriage feast at Cana was where the Lord performed the first miracle—turning water to wine. The water turning to wine in the communion goblet will remind us of miracles.

"then gifts of healing . . ."

As we look inside the wine goblet we see a small gift-wrapped package floating in the wine. As we look closely at it we see one end of it is bursting open. What do you think is in the package? Pushing its way out of the gift package is a bandaid ("gifts of healing").

"helps . . ."

Now as we continue to look at these yoked and stacked images the next part of our memory verse appears. We see jumping up and down on this package, this gift of healing floating in the wine goblet, a very tiny, tiny man. He is jumping up and down on the package as it floats around in the wine. This rather strange looking person represents "helps." What does helps look like? Helps is pictured as a carpenter or handyman perhaps, bib overalls, hammer hanging on the belt, perhaps a screwdriver, perhaps a saw in one hand. He clearly looks like a helper.

"governments . . ."

But he is jumping up and down not because he wants the exercise, but because he is attempting to reach the corner of a flag which is just out of his reach. This flag is hanging down so that just the tip of it is at the edge of the outstretched hands of our "helps." What does the flag stand for? The flag stands for "governments," the symbol to most of us for government.

"diversities of tongues . . ."

But as we look at the flag which is fluttering there in the breeze just out of reach of helps, we see a great number of tongues (that's correct—tongues!) sewn all over the flag. All the tongues are different colors: red, green, purple, yellow, blue. So as we look at that flag we not only see the flag but we see "diversities of tongues."

Now, Review

Now as you think back over this scripture verse and
the visualizing we have just done, you see that each
one of the items in I Corinthians 12:28 is touching the
next item (stacked and yoked). All that is necessary for
us to do to remember this scripture verse is to start with
the first item in the verse and in our mind's eye follow
it from item to item up the stack. You can even start
with the last item in the verse and go backwards down
the stack. You might try at this point quoting the scripture
verse that we have just memorized.

Quote it from memory but instead of starting at the
beginning, start by quoting from the end of the verse.
Think of the last image memorized in the verse: letting
it remind you of the words of the verse. Then work
your way back down the stack to the first of the scripture
verse. Can you do it? It would go something like this:
"diversities of tongues, governments, helps, gifts of healing, miracles, teachers, prophets, apostles, God hath set
some in the church." We have given concrete form to
some rather abstract concepts, and we have yoked each
item to the next item and have given it as much of a
stacking in our mind as is possible.

Remember, these images suggest the key phrases of
the verse. Polish and preciseness and accuracy come with
review of these images. Make certain that you concentrate

on the images enough so that you get the image-flow thoroughly fixed in your mind before you start translating the images into the actual verse. This way word for word accuracy is easily achievable.

What About the Chapter and Verse Reference?

Now how do you yoke the scripture reference to the verse? Merely take the book name (I Corinthians) and convert it to a visual image. Second, convert the chapter and verse references to the rhyme system number images. Third, yoke these book, chapter and verse images to the beginning or end of the verse just memorized. For instance, Corinthians is represented by a Corinthian column. Since this is First Corinthians we would have one column, Second Corinthians would have two columns. So it's one column with a rhyme word for 12 attached to it. Twelve is delve which is the bucket of the steam shovel. The steam shovel is resting on top of the column. The rhyme word for 28, the verse location of the scripture, is minty-bait. The visual image is a peppermint striped worm on a hook. The peppermint striped worm on the hook is inside the bucket which is resting on top of the Corinthian column which is balanced on top of the entire memory verse stack of images.

I suspect that if you were to give yourself one hour to do something else, or allow yourself time to think about other things and then come back to see whether you still remember this scripture verse, you would remember it easily. Using exaggeration, stacking and yoking you can very effectively memorize scripture.

Scripture Memorization with Others

These same scripture memorization techniques can be used very effectively with young people in a classroom or group situation. In this case, however, instead of you suggesting what the various word parts of the scripture verse should look like or be visualized as, you ask the class to suggest the key word or concrete image that best represents the part of the verse being memorized. You will find very quickly that nearly everyone visualizes basic concepts the same way. And this is especially true when you speak in terms of the basic visual images in the Bible. One of the nice things about memorizing scripture using this mnemonic technique is that once you come up with a visual image for an abstract idea you will never forget it and it will always be the same symbol that you'll use every time you want to remember that same concept.

For instance, whenever we think of salvation, most of us automatically think of the cross. Thus when you are memorizing a verse of scripture which has salvation as part of it, your visual symbol very quickly leaps into your mind as a cross. The same thing for love. When we think of love, we generally think of a heart. The heart then becomes the symbol for love. We never use the heart symbol for anything else other than the symbol of love.

As a group project, young people find great delight in speculating, discussing, and arguing over which is the best concrete symbol for abstract terms. Interestingly enough for most of the young people who memorize scripture this way, and for many adults, this group experience becomes the first time they ever really thought about the meaning of some of these concepts that we take for granted. Faith, hope and love become more than just words in the Bible.

6
Memorizing
and Study

ONE OF THE best uses for improved memory techniques is in studying difficult material. Whether it's the studying of a textbook you use in a college or high school course or studying material in preparation for a Bible study or sermon you are presenting, an improved memory can be dramatically beneficial.

The Best Time of the Day

There are, however, several things to keep in mind along with all that we have said so far about how our memory is improved. The first thing to keep in mind is that there is a good time of the day to try to study and there is a bad time. Educational psychologists have known for years that the best time of the day to study is quite early in the morning, probably somewhere between 7 and 9 A.M. This time of the day is ideal for

165

most people because generally they have had a good night's sleep, have eaten breakfast, and are at peak physical condition and mental alertness. Since the mind is clear and there are fewer physical demands on the body, the mind is capable of remembering more readily and of learning more rapidly.

The Worst Time of the Day

The worst time of the day to study is when most of us do ninety per cent of our reading and studying and that's in the evening. In fact, when studies were conducted to determine just how good a time the morning is for studying as compared with studying in the evening, there were some dramatic results. For instance, a person who studies between 7 and 9 in the morning and is tested on what he has learned is generally found to remember what may be called an average amount of factual information. However, that same person reading the same book from 7 till 9 in the evening and being tested will remember only about half as much as he did in the morning. It is simply that his mind is more fatigued toward the end of the day and recall will be more difficult. So don't stack the deck against yourself. Make sure that when you apply your memory training techniques, you do it at the best possible time of the day.

It has also been discovered that people cannot remember as well shortly after waking up as they do after they have been up long enough to get their mind functioning normally. A common experience when we are still groggy immediately upon waking in the morning is listening to the radio to hear the weather forecast for the day, but then two minutes after the forecast has been given, not being able to remember what the forecast was. Thousands of us wake up in the morning, put sugar in our coffee and then later have to taste the coffee to see whether we put sugar in it. When we are in a half drowsy condition, it is a waste of time to try to learn. Immediately upon waking in the morning is probably not the best time for daily devotions if your purpose is to contemplate and absorb God's truth. It is certainly not a good time to attempt to memorize a scripture verse.

Selectively Talk Aloud While Reading

Another good habit for memory development is the habit of selectively combining talking and reading. But, the key word is selectively. Talking, or vocalizing, while you're reading will slow you down as you read. It is, however, a good idea to talk to yourself as you read specific things you are trying to memorize. Although this will cause you to cover much less material than you would like to cover, there is a benefit for memorization. If you will repeat aloud what it is you wish to memorize as you read it and think it, you will find this combination of concentrated effort has a reinforcing effect on your mind. To do this all the time or to constantly talk while you are reading is to find that nothing significant happens for your memory. Selectively talking aloud to yourself will cause you to remember those things slightly better.

Reviewing at Bedtime

Another good time to try to remember things (to review what has previously been memorized or learned) is at bedtime. Bedtime is one of the best times to offset forgetting. It has been discovered that only 9% of what has been memorized in the forenoon can be recalled 8 hours later. But when that same material was reviewed at bedtime, approximately 56% of it could be recalled after 8 hours sleep.

When it comes to scripture memorization, this is especially significant. One of the best ways for the impact of the scripture to strike us is to read, memorize or review shortly before we go to bed. It is true that the thing that is in our mind just before we fall asleep is generally the first thing we think of in the morning when we wake up. Knowing this we should use the time just before we fall asleep to review that scripture passage that we have been memorizing. Thus in the morning we'll wake up and the scripture passage will be fresh and ready for us to contemplate for the day.

Learning While Asleep

It is extremely doubtful that you can learn while asleep. Experiments by psychologists and educational experimenters show that nothing is remembered from the so-called "sleep learning" techniques where a phonograph record or tape is played into our ears when we are in a deep sleep. Since there is no reaction from the mind there is no learning and certainly no memory. However, we do remember when we are awake but lying relaxed. We may even have our eyes closed, but can remember things though we are drowsy. When we are in this drowsy, near-sleep condition our reaction is slowed down, because we are not getting as much retention as possible under ideal circumstances. If we will open our eyes, look at what it is we want to remember, or concentrate on it intently, our reaction perks up.

Brushing Up

In memory training as in all other training, it is important to keep our memories sharp by brushing up occasionally. The person who uses his memory training abilities on a regular basis finds that he has a tendency to strengthen and develop his memory on a long term basis. Others, however, find that if they do not actively use memory training principles on everything they do, they will have a hard time keeping their memory abilities as strong as they can be. It is important for all of us but especially for these people to be constantly brushing up our memories so that they remain clear.

There are some general guidelines for keeping sharp which can be easily followed. The best time to brush up is immediately after you memorize the material. This helps cement the information and keep it clear. The next best time to brush up on your memory is at bedtime, just before you go to bed. It is also especially important to review during the first week or so after memorizing something.

What To Do When It Is Hard to Recall

But what do you do when it is hard to recall? There are several things. First, keep calm. If you get panicky or tense you have a tendency to forget even faster. The more relaxed you are, the easier it is to recall. Second, make an attempt to recall the original situation in which the forgotten information was used. We commonly forget people's names. One way to remember a name is to recall the original occasion when you met the person. Then try to remember all that happened, and probably the name will come. If you can visualize the actual sequence of events that led to the getting of the original information you should be able to lead yourself right up to the time when the original learning took place. This should help you recall the situation and the information. Sometimes it is very difficult to reinact the original situation where memorization took place. But if at all possible, act it out, actually talk with yourself as if you were two people, or play out whatever the situation was. This should cause you to remember.

Just Forget It

And finally even if you do not recall whatever it was, don't worry, just forget about it. That's right, forget about it. Relax, think about it for awhile and wait. You may be surprised, in the middle of the night the information that you were desperately trying to remember may suddenly wake you up and you recall it.

7
Remembering
Names and Faces

Why Is It Hard to Remember Names and Faces?

MEMORIZING NAMES and faces is usually very difficult for most of us. We generally have a tendency to forget names very quickly. For people involved in ministries that deal constantly with people it becomes increasingly important to remember names and be able to attach them to the right faces. Thus one of the things we have got to do in improving our ability to remember names and faces is to make a covenant with ourselves to intend to remember people we want to remember.

This means that when we are introduced to someone it's important for us to observe that person's face and to hear his name pronounced correctly if we are going to remember it. But instead of concentrating on seeing a person's face and hearing the name in order to remember the person's face, we very often are concerned with making our own good impression on him. We therefore

cannot remember either his face or his name because
we are thinking about ourselves. We're more concerned
with making a favorable impression than with impressing
the other man's name on our memory.

Intend to Remember

The first rule to observe when it comes to memorizing
names and faces is this: When meeting someone for the
first time, get him to talk about himself and then *intend*
to remember what he says. This may be done by asking
the person to remark about his interesting name or
occupation or perhaps mention something about his
clothing or some personal effects such as a ring or watch
that he is wearing. Then while he is impressing you
by talking about himself, look at the face with a view
of selecting something on which you can fix your attention. Forget about making a good impression on him.
There's not much you can do anyway.

Select a Prominent Feature

When it comes to selecting a prominent feature to use
as your reminder of that person in the future, look
carefully at the parts of the face. Every person has
something that is distinguished. For instance, a face may
be unusually large or small. Hair may be straight or

curly, or the person may be bald or partially bald. He
may have a high forehead or a prominent forehead. Or
he may have a straight nose, a large nose, or small one.
Eyebrows may be thick or bushy or even dramatically
curved. A person's eyes may be large or small, they may
be slanting or narrow. Ears may be prominent or tiny.
Teeth may be irregular or even super white. But whatever
it is, we must pick a prominent feature that will best
represent that person for us in the future.

Hear the Name and Create a Visual Image

After you have looked at the face and you have picked
the most prominent feature, you must hear the name
and then get it correctly, even have it spelled if necessary,
so that you can visualize it. Some names are visualized
easily because they remind you of the names of friends
or relatives or because of the implied meaning of the
name itself such as Mr. Small, or Mr. Green. Some names
remind you of famous people. As soon as you've got
the name, create a concrete visual image. That image
is then to be attached or yoked to the feature on his
face that you have selected as the most prominent feature.
After you have picked the common feature, visualized
the name, and then attached it to the feature, repeat the
name as much as possible while you are talking to the
person.

Remembering Groups of People

You can use this same approach for remembering groups of people. It's harder but it can be done. The secret is that you must meet the people in the group one at a time. This means that whenever you are introduced to 30 or 40 people, you, the memorizer, must set your own pace for being introduced. Generally this means you are introduced to each person one at a time in groups of two or three. After each small group of people, pause to mentally recall their names and the prominent feature that you have the name yoked to. Then meet several more people, once again to recollect their name and those you have met earlier. If by chance a name escapes you, go back and say to the person something like, "I'm sorry but I wanted to get your name right. What was the last name again?" Or, "How did you say it was spelled?" And just hope it wasn't spelled S-m-i-t-h or something like that. It is a basic Christian principle to be straight (honest) with people. I personally don't believe anyone is ever offended when I say, "It's important to me to get your name right. Will your repeat it for me?" I have even gone back 10 or 20 or 30 minutes later and have said, "Once more on your name—I am determined to get it right!" They are generally pleased with my interest. Never allow anyone to prevent you from setting your own pace as you introduce yourself to strangers. Don't let people throw you off or distract you or attempt to monopolize your attention. Remember, you are usually the stranger in the middle of the group. Chances are, they're more interested in impressing you than you should be in impressing them.

8
Memorization as a Group Function

Can Children Be Taught Memory Improvement Techniques?

C AN THE TECHNIQUES and principles that we have talked about so far be communicated to children in the family or perhaps even to the Sunday school class? Can memorization be fun? Can all ages, and large groups of people work together to develop improved memories? Yes. The smaller the child, the easier it is for him to imaginatively visualize things, and thus, the easier it is for him to picture concepts and stack and yoke. Large groups of people find it very entertaining to work together memorizing things. Each person's imagination has a tendency to stimulate the imaginations of the others in the group.

Memorizing with a Group

Scripture memorization can be a very exciting and stimulating experience for young people. One of the worst experiences for most of us in the past years has been when we have been required to memorize a weekly memory verse. Since a rote system was the only method we knew, memorizing Bible verses was always work. Now, relying upon the vivid imaginations of children, you can start them memorizing scripture easily and quickly. If you explain briefly what you know about how we memorize and then stress the ideas of stacking in one place, of yoking, and of how important it is to give concrete images to the things we want to remember, young people will take scripture memorization seriously and will concentrate on it as an enjoyable experience. In fact, one of the most exciting experiences for any Sunday school teacher is to work with young people who have just learned basic scripture memorization principles and who are beginning to visualize, stack and yoke scripture verses. You, the teacher, or the leader of the group, can serve as the guide as they memorize in suggesting which phrase or which idea in a verse comes next. Often, simply indicating with a question what the next phrase to be memorized is and then leading the students to agree among themselves how it is best visualized, will put the verse into concrete and easily remembered form. You'll find that the students find this scripture memorization experience extremely enjoyable. A Sunday school class with each person contributing to find the best visual image for the phrase or idea being expressed in the scripture can be stimulating for you also.

Even the small children in the family can memorize scripture quickly and effectively this way and find it enjoyable. Scripture memorization games around the dinner table in the evening can be exciting.

A CONCLUSION
AND A BEGINNING

Now that you have read this far you are certainly aware that an improved memory is not something that happens accidentally. On the contrary, an improved memory is something you *make* happen—and it can be made to happen fairly easily and with very little time investment. How do you get started?

First, review (from memory!) the basic principles and instructions in this book. Go back to the Table of Contents for an outline of the material covered and let it serve as a reminder for you. Anything that doesn't seem familiar, read again.

Next, apply the principles and methods immediately:

1. Why not spend fifteen minutes a day at a specific time each day actually memorizing? A good time each day might be at breakfast memorizing a short scripture passage with the family, or even on your lunch hour at work.

2. Move from single verse memorization of scripture to short passage memorization as your memory powers begin to develop. Increase the length of the passage from day to day. Remember to keep reviewing past passages. Fifteen minutes a day is still plenty of time for these longer passages because with practice you are able to memorize faster.

3. Share your new memory skills and techniques with a friend, your family, or your Sunday school class. Why not become a hero (for providing much needed help), a memory specialist (there really aren't enough of us in the world, you know), and a better prepared person (you will certainly be more knowledgeable and more trusted and respected for that evident knowledge). Also, the more you share what you have learned, the stronger you personally will become.

And finally, when you apply the techniques in this book and they bring help and blessing, tell me about it so that I can rejoice with you. A note or a card addressed to me in care of Quill Publications, 1260 Coast Village Circle, Santa Barbara, California 93108, will be appreciated. May the blessing of God's will and God's word be with you in a new way.